Calling All Parents

Sabrina Scott

Llumina
Press

© 2010 Sabrina Scott

ISBN: 978-1-60594-550-7 (PB)

Printed in the United States of America by Llumina Press

Library of Congress Control Number: 2010908363

Dedication

I dedicate this book to my mother Elizabeth Stokes: my rock, my role model and my #1 teacher. I thank you for showing me how to be a good loving mother, and for guiding, nurturing and protecting me with all of your love and support.

To my grandmother Elease Davis: I thank you for your inspirations, strengths, knowledge and faith and for introducing me to our father Jesus Christ whom I love and adore.

Acknowledgements

To my husband Corey for being in my corner and pushing me to get my book published. To my two boys: Omari and Christopher, for realizing the importance of education and for being respectable young men. Last but not least, my stepdaughter Korein our time together is always a pleasure.

Table of Contents

Introduction   i

Where It All Begins   1

Talk to Me   7

Not Easy   27

Where Is the Loyalty   37

Take Control   51

Teachers Can't Do It Alone   59

Calling All Parents

Introduction

*I*n this new millennium, it seems as if we are going backward in time instead of progressing. When I take a look at today's youth, who are supposed to be our future, I worry. Too many of our children are falling behind—academically and socially. They lack the knowledge they need to succeed in this world, and many lack social skills as well.

In the past few years, while working in the public schools as a substitute teacher, I have noticed that too many of our children seem angry. They are angry for various reasons: no father around, being poor, parents addicted to drugs who care more about supporting their habit than taking care of their children. This anger builds up inside our youth and is channeled out into the world. They seem upset at everyone and everything, because they are young and don't know how to control their anger, or how to release it safely. They carry all of their burdens on their backs until they eventually start dumping them on the world.

This anger hurts our youth in ways we can't imagine. One way is that it affects their schoolwork, and once children have fallen behind, they often feel that it is impossible to catch up. They give up, thinking that no one cares who they are or what they do. From that moment, you have the makings of another statistic: a killer, a rapist, a prostitute, a robber, or a drug dealer.

Allow me to introduce myself. I am a mother who is looking for a way to help our children get out of this angry, mad-at-the-world, don't care, have- no-respect-for-my-elders-or-myself attitude. I want to offer some suggestions that may help start the healing process that our children need.

While substitute teaching, I wanted to inspire as many young people as I could. If I just reached one child a day, I felt I was helping . . . but not fast enough. It saddened me to see how many children did not care about learning, and how many just went to school looking to see what kind of trouble they could get themselves into, just for attention. But what really disappointed me was seeing how many parents showed a lack of interest when teachers would reach out to communicate with them.

As a parent of two boys and one teenage stepdaughter, I am a firm believer that a child's behavior is a direct reflection of their parents or caregivers. They may not do what you did at their age, but they will do what you allow them to do. If children are given no direction, they will not know where to go. If children are not disciplined from the day they are born, there will be future problems.

Where It All Begins

It all starts from the day you bring your little bundle of joy home from the hospital for the very first time. Babies are so cute and irresistible you don't want to put them down, so you put your baby—let's say you have a boy—in the bed with you because you can't tear yourself away from him. Now your baby is so used to having you hold him that now you can't put him down without him crying. As soon as he makes that sad face, even before the crying begins, you are right there to give him what he wants, which is to be held. Days go by, weeks go by, and by the time a month comes around, you are drained.

You are now ready to just let your baby cry for a minute because you are so tired of getting up. His lungs are getting stronger now that he is getting older and his cries are getting louder, so you run to his rescue just to stop the noise, because you can't take it anymore. You pick him up, and suddenly the cries stop. He isn't hungry, he isn't wet or uncomfortable, he just wants to be held. Months go by and your baby is getting bigger and heavier. He's rolling over and taking up more and more space in your bed, so now you try to put him in his own bed, only to find that he will not stay. The crying starts all over again, this time louder and stronger, and you give in, despite your discomfort. He is now back in your bed with you again and is calm and relaxed, because he's where he wants to be. The crying stops, and he falls asleep.

Even at this young age, your child starts to realize that all he has to do is cry, and you will give in and he will get whatever he wants. As time goes by and he gets older, those cries begin to turn into tantrums:

yelling, screaming, throwing things, kicking, and hitting. I see this far too often in the grocery stores, at the mall, and even at restaurants. He does whatever it takes to get your attention because he knows that eventually you are going to give in and give him what he wants. After a few minutes of this outrageous behavior, he is right, you do succumb to him because not only are you exhausted but now you are embarrassed and you just want it all to be over.

Sometimes, especially when your little one is a baby and still learning, maybe it's not such a bad idea to let him cry for a while, if you've checked to make sure he doesn't need to be changed, doesn't have a fever, and isn't hungry. If you've been through the routine checklist, the only possible reason for your baby's discomfort is that you are not there holding him. He needs to realize that crying is not the answer. You need to teach him, even as a baby, that crying only gets him what he needs and not what he wants. As hard as it may seem, it will pay off in the long run.

I can remember getting upset with my husband because I was that mother who did not want to make my baby suffer. If he cried, I wanted to pick him up and comfort him. He was my first child, and I wanted to be the best mom to him that I possibly could be, but my husband would always tell me to leave him and let him cry. "It's good for his lungs" he would say, and I would get so upset that I had tears in my own eyes. It would absolutely kill me to listen to my baby cry his little heart out. My husband would tell me there was nothing wrong with him. "He's just eaten, he's not wet, he's just spoiled. All he wants is for you to pick him up." And we would argue, because I would always get defensive and say, "But what if something really *is* wrong with him and we don't know it. I mean, it is our first child, and we are not professionals at this parenting thing." So, I would pick him up in spite of how my husband felt, and guess what? The crying would stop immediately. So you know what I heard next? That's right: "I told you so." Well, eventually I did start to listen to my husband, because I knew my little baby was playing me. As hurtful as it was, I had to let him cry himself to sleep sometimes.

I must say, as hard as it was, I am very grateful to my husband for making me see the difference, because as time went on, I did not have to go through the temper tantrum stage. My child knew exactly how to behave outside the house, he knew that falling out on the floor screaming was not a way to get my attention or what he wanted, and he knew that crying and throwing things would not only get him in big trouble; he still would not get what he was hoping for.

Now that my firstborn is eleven years old with still a way to go before he is grown, he knows what is expected of him, and he know that communication is the way to express himself. If things don't go in his favor, sure, he will be upset for a while, but shortly afterward he'll get over it and try to understand why I said no. Or he'll come and ask me why, and we'll have a calm discussion about it.

Talk to Me

Sometimes children don't realize what they are asking for, so you need to explain it to them in a way they can understand. If we constantly yell at our children and say, "I said no, and that's that," without giving children any kind of explanation, they will be confused and think you're just being mean, when you may have a very good reason for saying no. You just never took the time to explain the reason.

Communication is important, no matter what your child's age. I've seen parents beat a child without telling the child what the punishment is for. Then when the child asks, "What did I do?" the parent says, "You know what you did." But they may not know at all. They may have done something that was wrong in the parents' eyes, but right in their eyes, and may have seen nothing wrong with what they did. So you should first find out if children understand what they did, and whether they did it deliberately or accidentally, or if they simply did not know any better. Talk to your children. It could make a world of a difference. You can turn a mistake into a learning opportunity, instead of teaching that violence is the way to correct mistakes.

I am so thankful to my husband for what he showed me. I know that not everyone has a husband or significant other around to help with these things. That is why I wanted to write this book. I want to share my personal experiences in the hope that it will make a change, if only in a few households at a time. I am not saying my method works for everyone; all I am saying is give it a try, and maybe, just maybe, it will help in your situation as well. I want to help those who are looking for help in any way I possibly can, because parenting is not an easy job.

Every day is a new learning experience, and you just have to keep up with it. I followed those same guidelines with my second son, and he does not throw tantrums either. He is nine years old now, and if I have to tell him he can't have something he wants, he will be upset, but he will understand and will be able to tell you why I said no, because I try to keep the line of communication open in my household. We discuss everything in great detail, to ensure that everyone understands, and there is no confusion. He may not agree with my decision, but he will know *why* I made that decision.

Let me give you an example of what I am talking about. My kids are not allowed to play video games during the school year unless they are on an extended vacation, for instance, spring break, when they are home for five or more consecutive days. The reason I felt the need to limit their game playing to vacation time is I found that when I used to let them play on the weekends, my oldest son would be in school all week and his whole focus would be, "I can't wait until Friday so I can play the game." So let me ask you, if he is in school on Tuesday worrying about Friday, is he really paying attention to his teacher and his class work? I think not! That's why I had to take that distraction away from him. He, of course, did not like what I did, but he understands that in my house, school is to be his main focus, not video games, and the improvement in his grades tells me that I made the right decision.

Children need someone to guide them. They like to have organization and rules to follow, whether we realize it or not. It makes them feel comfortable, and it gives them something to look forward to. They need order and consistency in their daily lives, because it will play a major role in their growing up. Without it, they will be all over the place trying to find where they fit in. They need to know from the beginning what is expected of them, and they need to know what is appropriate behavior and what is not.

When I say a child needs discipline, I'm not talking about being physical. That just tells them that violence is the way to get your point across. There are other ways to discipline your children without physically harming them. For example, restricting them from their favorite activities— sports, television, or talking to their friends on the telephone. Taking away your child's favorite thing will hurt more than any beating you can give. Today, if you take your child's cell phone away, for instance, she will be at your mercy. Trust me. Children think they can't live without it. When you take something away, you have to keep it for a while to let them know how serious you are, and to let them know that you mean what you say. If you give it back too soon, they will not take you seriously. Sometimes this punishment hurts us more than it hurts them, because it is hard to see them cry, but you have to teach them that there are consequences for wrongful actions.

Bottom line, find a form of discipline that you're comfortable with and stick to it, no matter what. If there are two parents in the household, you both have to be on the same page with the discipline, at least in front of the children. Don't let them see or hear you disagreeing, because they will turn that to their favor, and they will go to whomever they consider the weaker parent to try to get what they want. If you disagree with the way your partner is handling a situation, hold that thought. When the children are not around, you can discuss it quietly at another time and place.

As for all the single parents out there, I know it's hard. I can't say I know exactly how you feel, because I haven't walked in your shoes, but having grown up in a single parent home with seven siblings, I can understand your struggle. My mother never made us feel as if we were missing out on anything because our father was not around. She did all she could to support us. It may not have seemed like much to others, but whatever she did for us and whatever she gave us meant the world to us, because we knew she didn't have any extra money to spent on luxury items, such as fashionable clothing to keep up with the other children in school. But it didn't matter to us. We made the best of what we had.

I can remember how excited I was when my mother would come home from work, because she always had something in her bag for me. It could have been cheese and crackers from the vending machine at her job or a pack of gum or new clips for my hair—things that may seem frivolous to others were such a huge comfort to me. I felt like the luckiest child in the world, because I knew that even while she was at work, my mom always thought about me.

So what if you can't buy your son those Jordan's he wants so badly, or the new Barbie doll your daughter asked you for. Sometimes even children can understand the struggle, if you sit them down and explain it to them. It teaches them to appreciate the finer things in life. It teaches them that life is not all about glitz and glamour, especially for middle class or poor families who are not able to afford some of the material things that their friends may have.

I don't know how different it would have been to have my father in the house, but I wouldn't trade my childhood and my family's struggle for the world. My mom was a hard working mother who came home from work, cooked dinner every night, and still found time to sit down and have conversations with us to find out what our day was like. She even went to the PTA meetings to see how we were doing in school, and she knew where we were at all times. And yes, she disciplined us as well. And you know what? I love her for that, and I appreciate everything she did for my family and me.

It is important for a single parent to make time for the children, because it's not only you who are struggling. Your child is struggling, too. You have to play the role of both parents. You have to be soft, loving, and kind; you have to cook, clean, and help with homework, like other moms do, all while being firm, administering discipline, and being as tough as some fathers are. It's a hard task, but not impossible. Single parents are the ultimate multi-taskers, and are severely underpaid. I salute those who are giving it their best shot. But for those of you who want to give up, I say find a support group that can help you talk out your frustrations. You are not alone in this; there are many other single parents who find it extremely difficult to deal with their children.

Although it may seem like an uphill battle sometimes, seeing your young child grow up to be a successful, loving, responsible adult will make all your struggles worthwhile. Keep at it. Don't give up on your child. After all, your child is a product of you. If you have older children, let them help you with the younger ones. I'm not saying they should constantly be responsible for their younger siblings, but they should be able to offer some help when you need it.

As the youngest of eight children, I not only had to answer to my mother, but to my older sisters as well. They would discipline me, or they would tell on me, so either way I was going to be in trouble if I got out of line.

When I was in elementary school I used to hate going to school so much that my mother bought me a shirt with the words "I love school" printed on the front. I asked her, "Why did you buy me a shirt like this? You know that's not true. All my friends and even my teacher are going to laugh at me because they all know it's not true, too." She smiled and told me to turn the shirt around, and when I read the back, I laughed so hard I had tears in my eyes. The back of the shirt read, "when it's closed." I proudly wore my "I love school when it's closed" shirt to school the very next day.

As much as I didn't like school, I knew I had no choice but to go every day, or I would be in trouble. My school was right around the corner, so by the time I was in the fourth grade, no one had to escort me anymore. I was a big girl now, and my mother trusted me to go to school by myself and be there on time.

My mother always left for work fifteen minutes after I left for school. She had to catch the bus on the corner of our street, going in the same direction I took to go to school. One Monday morning I decided I was not going to go to school, so I tried to act as if I was not feeling well. But she was not going for it, and she told me I had better be out of the house before she had to leave for work.

The morning dragged on as I got myself ready for school. Mom walked me to the door, gave me a kiss, and said, "Have a good day." Tears were now rolling down my face, my head hung low, and I walked slowly out of the door. As I walked toward the corner, a bright idea popped into my head. The corner house was surrounded by very tall bushes, so I thought I could hide in the bushes until I saw my mother pass by to catch her bus. About ten minutes later, there she was, walking right past me. I was very quiet and still to ensure that she would not notice me, and she didn't. *It worked,* I thought to myself, *it worked*. I was so happy! I stayed there until the bus came and she was on her way to work.

Once my mother was safely on her way, I ran back into the house and up the stairs into my room and hid in my closet, because one of my sisters was still home, and I didn't want her to see me. I stayed in the closet for about fifteen minutes before I heard my sister leave the house. I finally came out the closet and went downstairs to watch cartoons, thinking I was safe . . . when my sister came back in because she had forgotten something. She opened the door, and we were both startled. For a split second, she thought I was an intruder, and I thought, *oh, no, I'm in trouble.*

"What are you doing home," she yelled. I tried to explain to her that I was not feeling well, but she knew I was up to the same old tricks, trying to get out of going to school. "As soon as Mommy gets to work, I'm calling her and telling her what you did." Thank goodness there were no cell phones back then; otherwise my mother would have gotten off that bus immediately. I begged and pleaded with my sister not to tell, but she would not have it any other way. Sure enough, at 9:01 she was on the telephone with my mother. Can you believe that little snitch? I was so upset at her, but she didn't care, because she knew she had to be responsible enough to do what was right. She knew it wasn't a good thing that I had tricked my mother and cut school.

If it wasn't for my sisters and brothers helping out, I probably would have been an elementary school dropout! That's how much I did not like going to school.

Sometimes it takes more than just the parents to raise a child. Sure, I was mad at my sister back then, but I sure am glad she didn't let me mess up my future so early in my life. Eventually, when I saw I had no one on my side who was going to let me get away with skipping school, I gave up the fight. I graduated from high school with a 3.5 grade point average and went on to earn my bachelor's degree. So, I say thank you to my sisters and brothers for caring about my future.

Don't let your surroundings determine your worth. You may live in the projects, but that does not mean you should give up on your hopes and dreams of someday becoming successful. Don't let negative stereotypes keep you down. Always strive to be the best you possibly can be. Everyone has a hidden talent; you just have to dig deep to find what yours is. Some people draw conclusions about you when you say you are from the projects or the "ghetto." They immediately think of drugs and crime, which is not always the case. There are educated, focused individuals who dwell right in your hood, and you are probably one of them. Sure, others may call you names and tease you for trying to better yourself, but once you are on top, those same people will respect and admire you and wish they were as strong as you.

Don't get lost and wrapped up in the drug scene, because it only jeopardizes your well-being and your child's well-being. If you take your children to the crack house with your from the time they are born until they are school age, what have you taught them, other than how to get high? They say the most important part of a child's life is his first few years. This is when a child watches your every move, to learn from you. It is critical to show positive things, rather than negative things. These images stay with children longer than you may know.

If your child is growing up watching his parent(s) get high on alcohol or drugs, he may have less respect for you, your friends, or the dealers who sell to you. These are all adults your young child will not respect. If you continue this behavior in front of the child, and this lifestyle has completely consumed your life, by the time your child is ten years old, he is so angry with you and the crazy world he lives in that he begins to develop self-hatred. He has no faith in a higher being, he's too embarrassed to tell anyone what is going on in his home, he has no friends, because he's too ashamed to bring anyone to his house, so he becomes a lonely, confused, tormented child. If by the time he is fifteen he goes on a killing rampage, you ask yourself why.

You were so busy getting high that you had no time to take him to school. He's missed so many days and fallen so far behind that now he doesn't even go to school anymore. He has now become that which you exposed him to his whole life. You gave him a drug dealer as a mentor and now, that's what he is—a drug dealer. After all, he has to support himself somehow, because he can't depend on you. It's a sad situation, but unfortunately, it's reality for some of our children today.

If we disrespect ourselves in front of our children, how can we possibly expect them to respect us? If we have no dignity or self-discipline, how do we expect our children to develop these qualities? We have to start setting positive goals and creating a positive atmosphere for our children in order for them to move forward in a positive way. It all starts in the home—not in school, not at a friend's house, not at the park—at home! It's time we stop passing the blame and take responsibility for the kind of children we raise.

There is a time and place for everything. If you are with your children, that is not the time for you to get drunk or high, or to let every other word that comes out your mouth be a curse word. Mothers should also dress respectably when around their children. You just don't want to send your child the wrong message. I'm not saying once you become a parent you have to stop being yourself; I'm just saying tone it down a bit when they are in your presence. Now, if you are out with your friends, that's your time and you should do as you please. But when your children are around, their best interest should come first. I have seen mothers at the movie theater with their children, wearing stiletto heels and the shortest possible mini-skirts. We have to know what is appropriate and what is not before we can teach our children the difference. We should wear respectable clothing while out with our children and carry ourselves in a respectable manner. If we don't respect ourselves, how can we expect our children to respect us?

If you prepare your children for what's in the streets by teaching them what's right and what's wrong, and build strength in your children, then no matter what they face in this world, they will be able to handle it and make the right decisions. Before they go out into this world they should know what is expected of them. They should know that you are not okay with them running with the "wrong" crowd. They should have enough respect for you that they will not want to break your heart and go against everything you have taught them.

We have to get back to encouraging our children and loving our children. We have to set goals and achieve those goals and make a difference. We have to stay in control at all times. Our youth are in trouble, and they need your parental guidance. That's why I'm calling on all parents to get involved and to take the time to reconnect with your children. It's not too late to regain control and lead them down the right path. You will be surprised how many of our children want us to step up and show them that we care. A lot of them are begging for love and attention because they have been neglected for so long; it's like a void in their hearts that needs to be filled. It's time we stop being selfish, trying to get back our own youth, and take care of our children. If you don't guide them, where will they go? Stop trying to be your children's best friend and be their parent. There's a time to play and a time to be serious, and your children should know what time it is.

Not Easy

I have been married for thirteen years to a wonderful man; however, just because their father lives at home does not mean it has been easy for me to raise my children. There have been plenty of arguments because he worked late at night for many years, coming home at nine or ten o'clock at night—five, sometimes six nights a week. I felt like a single parent trapped in a marriage, because he was never around to help me raise our children. He was not there when it was time to do homework, take them to the park, or break up fights between our two boys. I had to handle it by myself, all while trying to cook dinner and clean the house—after I came home from work.

I was stressed and upset, and I often felt that it was not fair. I wanted to give up. I thought about leaving him and my kids; that's how bad I felt. When you feel like you have reached the point where you can't take it anymore, seek help. Find ways to help reduce the stress, which angers or frustrates you. Some parents find it relaxing to do yoga even if it's only for five minutes, while others may lock themselves in the bathroom just to find time to regroup and calm down. As for myself, I would go into my room, close the door, sit on the floor with my eyes closed and take deep breaths until I felt relaxed enough to deal with my situation in a positive way.

It was at that time that I continually complained to him that it was not enough for him to just go to work and bring home the money; I needed a partner, someone to help me with everything around the house, and I needed help raising our children.

It was a long time before he got it out of his head that a man's job is to go to work and bring home the bread while the woman takes care of home. I had to let him know that this is a new day and age, and I worked just as hard as he did. I was not a housewife, and he had to get with the new times.

After missing a big part of his childrens' lives—first birthdays, their first steps, first words—he started to realize why I had been complaining so much. On the verge of losing everything—his wife and his children—he spoke to his manager about changing his hours so he could be home at a reasonable hour to spend time with his family, before it was too late.

I only had a tease of what it's like being a single parent, if I can even call it that, so I can only imagine how difficult it must be for the parents who do it every day with no help at all.

When we decide to become parents, no matter how old or young we are, the very moment our first child is born, life changes forever. We must become responsible adults, in order to give our children what they need. If you used to go out partying every other night or every weekend, guess what? That's going to have to stop. You have to make major sacrifices for a child, whether you are ready to or not.

No one is responsible for your children but you, not your mother, your father, your sister, or your aunt. No one should be raising your children while you are out running around in the streets. Being a parent means limiting your entertainment time away from home to maybe once a week, not three times a week, so you can bond with your children. If you are always out and away from your children and always leave them with their grandmother, your children are going to have a stronger bond with her than they will with you, so when your children call Grandma "Mommy," don't get upset; if you were there for them like you should be, that would not happen.

Many of us think of taking the easy way out by letting go of our family, getting a divorce, or putting our kids in foster care or up for adoption, but that is not the answer to the problems we face as parents. It only makes life harder for the children, in most cases. It puts too many questions in the children's minds, like why did my parents give up on me? This challenge for us is to work through our pain and suffering and deal with the situation at hand.

Parenting is the most difficult job in the world. There is no practice book or study guide. You just have to jump into it and give it your best shot keeping your children's best interests at heart at all times. As long as you are up for the challenge, you will make it through. It may not be a newly paved road you're going to go down, but you can make it through. And when the struggle is over and your children are grown, you will have plenty of stories and, hopefully, laughs to share when you tell your children about the heartache and pain they put you through over the years.

No one ever promised that life would be an easy road to travel, but we have to be strong and overcome any obstacles that may be thrown in our way. I know my struggles have made me stronger. I hope yours do the same for you.

If you choose to give up on your family and walk away, all you are teaching your children is when the going gets tough, give up! Is that really the message you want to send? Nothing in life is easy. Life is one big challenge after another, and worse than a failure is someone who doesn't even try. Adults get over broken hearts all the time, but for children it is much harder to understand why their father or mother doesn't want anything to do with them, and sometimes that question remains in their minds for the rest of their lives.

I know in my situation, I still sometimes feel a void from just not understanding why my father gave up on me. My father never tried to maintain a relationship with me, and to this day I don't know what his reasons were. I know sometimes some mothers make it extremely difficult for a father to see his children because every time he calls or comes around she harasses him for money or child support. Yes, it's his responsibility to help with this children's upkeep, but sometimes I think the mother should just give it a rest and let him spend quality time with his children, even if he has no money to give.

And to you fathers, even if the mother is making it difficult for you, I still say don't give up. Fight for visitation rights and show your children that you do want to be in their lives. It makes a difference to children. Don't make your child suffer for the other parent's actions. Don't give up the right to see your children and to spend quality time with them because you are having financial difficulties.

Both parents should try to maintain some kind of working relationship with each other for their children's sake. We all need a break sometimes from the stress of parenting, and when you have the opportunity to let your children spend time with the other parent, it not only gives you a break, but the children benefit from having both parents in their life. Sometimes mothers don't have all the answers for their sons, and they need a male perspective on certain topics, and sometimes girls want and need to feel like daddy's little princess. Maybe if more girls had their fathers around, they wouldn't try to grow up so fast and find a boyfriend to fulfill the need for a father figure, or look for any man to love them to fill the void in their hearts.

There are plenty of single parents out there who are raising their children very well, and again I commend you. But I'm sure even you can use a break sometimes and wouldn't mind having someone share the responsibility. I really don't understand why some women give men a hard time when they are putting forth the effort to help out. I have witnessed good men, men who were trying to do right by their children and be there for them, supporting them as best as they could, and it still was not enough for the woman.

In one situation I am familiar with, a man sent the mother of his child money orders every two weeks to help with his child's upkeep—money that she agreed to accept from him without going through the court system. He kept up his end of the bargain, but she decided somewhere along the way that she wanted more, so she decided not to cash any of the money orders. She took him to court for child support and told the judge that he had not given her any money at all. He thankfully had all of his money order receipts to prove he was sending her what he thought they had agreed upon. She thought for some reason she could get more money from him by going through the court system, and it turned out that he was ordered to pay her less than what he was sending her, so her scheme did not work in her favor at all.

If you have a child's father who is willing to work with you, why are you still bitter and trying to cause all kinds of problems? You need to let go of the past and your bitterness. Move on with your life, and let that man take care of his child. If he is not a deadbeat dad trying to avoid paying for his child, why cause problems when there are none?

Where Is the Loyalty

You have been dating someone for almost a year now and things are getting serious, you start to think this may be "the one." You decide to bring him/her home to meet your children, only to find out that your children do not approve. They don't like your mate's attitude, appearance, or demeanor, so your children tell you how they feel. You immediately go into defensive mode, because this person is who you have chosen to be with and want to spend the rest of your life with.

Time goes on, and the situation gets worse between your lover and your children, and you are caught in the middle. You constantly try to keep common ground and try to find solutions for them to come together, but in spite of all your efforts, they are just not getting along. The time has come when your relationship has grown into a proposal of marriage. What do you do? This will mean your children and your lover living together under the same roof. How will this ever work out?

As you have a family discussion about the situation at hand, your children object strenuously because no way do they want this person as a stepparent. They don't trust the person, and they think this person is a danger to the family given their past history. As the parent, you feel that it's not up to your child to decide whom you can and cannot marry, so you decide to marry this person anyway.

In a situation such as this, I would suggest that all of you get some family counseling before the marriage takes place. There obviously are some issues that need to be addressed in order for this union to work. Just because your children are minors does not mean they can't have valid viewpoints. For instance, if your child has witnessed this individual being violent toward anyone, either verbally or physically, and feels threatened, then maybe you should listen—for everyone's safety. No child should be put in a dangerous situation, and no adult should accept any form of abuse.

A person who loves you will not belittle you or put his hands on you. One time is one time too many for someone to abuse you, no matter what the situation may be, no matter how many times that person apologizes.

It's better to be safe now than sorry later. If a child feels this strongly against your mate, maybe you should reconsider. You don't want to choose a lover over your own child, who may never forgive you if you do.

I have a friend who told her nineteen-year-old son that if he didn't like the man she chose to marry, he could move out. How could a mother find it in her heart to put her own child out of the house over a man? And this happens to be her only child. What will happen if this marriage doesn't work out? How could you ever live with the fact that you turned your back on your own flesh and blood for someone who didn't appreciate it? How do you think this will affect your teenager? In a negative way, that's how.

When a child does not feel loved by his parents, that child will either not be able to show love for anyone, or will look for love in the streets or wherever it can be found, by hanging out with the wrong crowd. Children who do not feel love at home often attach themselves to anyone who shows them love, whether it's a pimp or a gang. They become vulnerable to those who prey on youngsters lacking direction and guidance and who are looking for a "new family."

If we start putting our children first and giving them the love, respect, and attention that they require, maybe we will eliminate some of the hatred in the world today. We have to take the time to listen to our children and hear their cries. We have to talk to them and give them the chance to express themselves. You know, sometimes they have very valid points and make more sense than some of you adults, but they are too often ignored because they are minors. We adults always like to tell them to be quiet because they don't know what's best for them. Give them the opportunity to communicate with you before you shut them down. You just may be surprised at how intelligent and mature your child has become.

Having positive role models around your children is always helpful if the role models are influential in a good way, but on the flip side, having a negative role model will be harmful, and your children may be influenced in a bad way. You may not want someone who will sit and watch the television show *Jackass* with your eleven-year-old, or pornography for that matter, and you may not want someone who can't have a conversation around your child without every other word being a curse word. This behavior may negatively impact your child's life, and I know there isn't one parent out there who actually wants that for his or her children. You have to be careful whom you bring around your children at all times.

I know it's hard to live your own life while trying to be a good parent, especially when you are still young yourself, or just young at heart. Some single parents enjoy the single life—meeting and dating different people all the time—and sometimes they feel like that person may be "the one," or maybe they just want to entertain their dates. Children immediately form an opinion about anyone a parent brings home, and we all know that first impressions are the most important ones. Sometimes the children are holding on to hopes that their parents will eventually get back together and be a happy family again, so they refuse to accept anyone else in their lives. They see the possibility that this new person will replace their real father or mother. The presence of the new person crushes their hopes and dreams.

My husband had a two-year-old daughter when I met him, but even though he was no longer with her mother, I still didn't meet her until two years later, when she was four years old, because he didn't want to bring me into her life if I was only going to be there for a short time and not for the rest of her life.

If you come into a child's life as a stepparent when the child is very young, it gives the child time to grow into you and get to know you before starting to judge you. When a child is too young to fully understand what is going on, it is less confusing than having you come into his or her life during adolescence. Children at this stage already have minds of their own. If they have met and grown attached to five other people before you, because their mother moved every man she ever dated into their home, and a couple of months later realized he wasn't the one for her, they will probably resist forming more attachments.

When children don't see consistency in your life, they may not only start to disrespect anyone else you bring home, but they may start to lose respect for you as well. That's why my husband wanted to make sure our relationship was stable and strong enough before he introduced me to his daughter. He wanted me to be the first and only other woman in her life, outside of her mother, that she would meet and grow to love. Now, I'm sure there were other women after he left his daughter's mother and before he met me, but none of them were around his daughter. He kept his personal life separate from her, because he didn't want to confuse her or break her heart. He knew these women would not be around for very long, and he didn't want her getting attached to someone he knew was only in his life temporarily.

You have to watch the company you keep around your children, because they learn from anyone who is directly involved in their daily lives, and look to them for guidance and understanding. So if you're dating someone who sells narcotics and thinks that's the only way to make it in this world, or someone who is fresh out of jail for murdering a neighbor, that may not be such a good choice to bring home for your children to meet. Yes, everyone should be given a second chance. But if you are giving a person the chance to prove to you that he or she has changed, keep that person away from your children, outside of your home. Your children do not need to meet everybody you date, because no one ever knows what a person is really like on the first date or even the first few dates. Sometimes it takes months or even years to really get to know someone. You may find out after dating someone for eight months that he is a child molester, or that he physically abused his last three girlfriends, so you decide to leave him before he has a relapse and abuses you. Won't you feel better saying "I'm so glad I never bought him around my babies and put them in that kind of danger"? I know I would.

Our children should not be taught (or brainwashed) that being a drug dealer is a life they should want because of all the money you can make. Sure, that fast life and fast money may look tempting, but is it worth it when you're sitting in jail, or when you are shot dead in the streets? The life of a hustler is not a career to which your young child should aspire.

We have to want more for our children. They should learn from our mistakes, not repeat them. We have to teach them right from wrong, and to show respect for others and for themselves. I know I'm repeating myself on this, but that's because I want it to get through to some of you. Our children's future is looking more and more like a disaster waiting to happen, and the world will continue to be filled with uneducated street bangers and killers if we don't change our ways.

We have to go back to the time when everyone understood that it takes a village to raise a child, not just the parents. It's time for all adults to stand up and voice their concerns when they see youngsters doing wrong. We have to stop turning the other cheek and fearing these kids, because they need our help. I don't know what happened, but my mother or the other adults in my neighborhood were never afraid of the children in the neighborhood. It was the other way around, because the adults all stood together and helped raise each other's children. If my neighbor saw me in the streets doing something I had no business doing, like cursing, smoking, or disrespecting my elders, she would not only embarrass me and chastise me, but she would also tell on me, which would get me into even more trouble.

Nowadays, it seems as if everybody is for themselves, everybody wants to ignore the problems around them, for fear of their lives or to avoid confrontations with our youth. I know it can sometimes be dangerous out there. You never know what is on someone's mind and you don't know if a young person has a weapon or not; but if you continue to ignore the situation, it can only become worse. I can recall my husband telling me about a time when he was going to the library to return a Sista Soulja book that he borrowed. In the parking lot of the library, a group of teenagers were hanging out. When an older man and his small child were passing the group, the man spoke to them with a simple hello, and one of the young girls yelled out "f*** off" to the man, for no apparent reason—or maybe to impress her friends. My husband could not believe what he'd just witnessed, so he immediately responded: "Was that really necessary?" The girl replied, "I was just joking with him," so my husband told her that it wasn't funny and she should show a little more respect for herself and others.

After hearing his story, I'll admit I was on the fence a little with his reaction, because anything could have happened; any one of those kids could very well have had a gun and shot him for not minding his own business. But I commended him, because that is exactly what we need to start doing. Who knows what that girl did after that situation? She may have gone somewhere else and caused other problems, but on the other hand, maybe. . . just maybe he got through to her. Maybe she realized that she had been wrong and decided never to act this way again. All I'm saying is that if everyone were to intervene and show our young people that we care about what is going on, maybe we would make a difference and turn things around for the better.

Just imagine where we would be if Dr. Martin Luther King, Jr. had given up on us and decided he wasn't going to speak out for us so we could live in equality, or if he decided to keep his "dream" to himself. Need I remind you how far we have come since then? Just to name a few examples, we have been celebrating the success of Bill Cosby and *The Cosby Show*, Oprah Winfrey being one of the richest women in America, Denzel Washington winning Grammy Awards, and Barack Obama becoming the forty-fourth president of the United States. So don't tell me getting involved is not going to work. We all need to think a little more like Dr. King and stand up for what is right. Enough is enough, and change has to come right now.

I strongly agree with the old saying "If you are not part of the solution, you are part of the problem." Whatever happened to the people who believe "united we stand, divided we fall?" Well, that's exactly what is happening— we are falling apart because no one wants to stand together. It seems as though no one has love in their hearts anymore. We need to eliminate all the negative vibes and bring in positive ones before we have a war against each other and self-destruct. It is sickening to turn on the news or read the newspaper only to hear about another teenager being shot or arrested. Our children need to know that there are other opportunities besides living the life of a criminal. They need to know that there's much more out there if they only look. It is up to us, the adults, to guide them in the right direction.

Take Control

Children need positive role models, and they need good things to look forward to in today's harsh world. They need to observe and be around people who have succeeded in life—people who had risen from the bottom and made it to the top. They need to hear from those people who started out going down the wrong path, but realized they needed to go the opposite direction to make something of themselves. There are a lot of people out there who think the world owes them something. It is your job as a parent to try your best to keep those people out of your children's circle. It is your job to know whether or not your child is old enough or mature enough to understand that although Uncle Joe is their uncle, unfortunately he is not someone they should emulate.

As a parent, you have to get to know your children and their maturity level. You should know whether a fifteen-year-old child is mature enough to watch a movie like *Monsters' Ball.* Some kids mature faster than others and may be able to follow the message in the storyline, while others may not be able to see past the sexual engagements that go on in the movie. As the parent and adult, it is up to your discretion to make that call.

If your child is immature for his age, then by all means please use the parental controls that are on your television sets and computers. You don't want to expose your children to something you know they are not ready for. Don't let the media raise your children. You have to set the pace, stay in control, and be responsible for what goes on in your home *and* how your child behaves outside of your home. Letting your children watch music videos all evening where Mariah Carey is prancing around in lingerie with her boobs pushed up and protruding out of her bra may not be a good thing for your eleven-year-old son to watch. I love Mariah Carey's music, but I will not watch her videos with my children, nor will I allow them to watch them at any time. I feel kids are exposed to way more than they can handle or are ready for.

Psychiatrist Daniel Amen, founder of Amen Clinics, said on an MSNBC show, *About Our Children,* "Children's brains don't finish developing until around the age of twenty to twenty-five years old, and until that time, they need good supervision." That's why it is so important for parents to stay informed about what their children are doing, and should use parental controls. Adolescents don't need to be exposed to sex and sexual behavior on TV or on the radio. That is not what they need to be focused on at such a young age.

It is a good idea to get into the habit of limiting the amount of time your children can watch television, go on the computer, or play video games, especially during the school year when they should be focusing on their studies. Turn off the television sometimes and read a book, the newspaper, or a magazine with your children to help stimulate their minds with something other than the violence and nudity that is all over the media. Children learn from example, and if they see Mom or Dad reading the paper or a book, they are bound to pick up a piece of reading material themselves at some point. If you make it part of your routine to read every night, before you go to bed or after dinner, instead of watching television, they might not depend on the television as much for entertainment.

Parents, you have to give your children more of yourselves; that means when you get home from work or when they come home from school, interact with them, talk to them, help them with their homework so you can know what areas they need help in. I cannot stress enough the importance of helping your children with their homework. It may only take you thirty minutes a day, maybe less, but it will have such a huge impact on your children's learning progress and development. Play family games with them, go out for dinner once in a while as a family, or have a family picnic outdoors or indoors if you can't afford to go to a restaurant. Do this without the television on, and I guarantee you will learn something about your children that you did not already know, or you will see a difference in your children's behavior and attitude. They will seem much happier and calmer, and they will feel the connection with you and won't be afraid to come and talk to you about anything. This not only builds a bond between parents and their children, but also friendship, which is just as important.

Start as early in life as possible showing your children love and attention, but know that it's never too late. Children will always need and love their parents, so it doesn't matter if they are two years old or twelve; they will appreciate and welcome a positive change in their lives. There are too many angry children out there today, feeling as if no one loves them, cares for them, or pays attention to them, so they end up getting themselves in trouble, trying to find anyone who will show them the slightest bit of attention, whether it's good or bad. They need us. How can we turn our backs on them? They need to be walked down a straight line with our guiding hands. Reach out and save our children, for they are going astray.

Parents today need to wake up, straighten up, and get our lives together. Remember, you are the one teaching your children. You need to show them how to act, how to behave in the streets, and how to show respect and maturity at all times, especially in public. You have to watch what you say and what you do around them, because they are constantly watching you in order to learn from you. If your children see you being respectful to others around you, carrying yourself in a mature manner, and using an educated vocabulary in your everyday speech, avoiding foul language at all times, that is what they will learn and follow.

If you don't agree with what I am saying, give it a try. Change the way you live your life around your children and see if there is a difference. Start initiating some ground rules and discipline in your home, even if you feel your children are too far gone and can't be reached. Give it a try anyway, because I don't think it's too late. As long as they are still adolescents, they still need you. If you feel you can't or don't want to do it alone, seek professional help for out-of-control children or teens. Talk to neighbors who may be going through the same or similar issues as you are, form a support group, or join one that is already in progress. Check for support systems online or through you local library.

Many parents have lost control of their children and are looking for solutions. Don't think you are alone, because I see it everyday at the schools where I work. I see parents coming to pick up their children or drop them off and their children are telling them what they will and will not do. I know right away that the children are running that household, and not the parent. Forget about what has gone on in the past and concentrate on the future. If you want it to be a positive one, then change has to happen, and it must be initiated immediately.

Whether you realize it or not, children need authority figures in their lives. They rely on us as adults and parents to keep order in the house, and they thrive on organization in their lives. Even if they don't agree with your rules, believe me, they will still follow them if you stand strongly behind what you say. Eventually, they will get so used to the routine that it will no longer be a big issue. You just have to get past the initiation part of it.

Teachers Can't Do It Alone

When children lack discipline at home, it shows at school. They leave their uncontrollable home and go to a school where there are rules they must follow, and they become confused, because that's not what they are used to. But guess what . . . the teachers and principals stick to their rules, regardless of how long it takes for your child to get used to them and accept them. Why not do the same at home? It is not 100 percent up to the school or teacher to teach your child respect and discipline. This must start at home. Children should enter school or daycare already knowing what is expected of them. They should already know that when the teacher or an adult speaks to them, they are to listen. Teachers are not babysitters; they should not have to constantly monitor and address your child's behavior. You should not be afraid of your child or afraid to set rules and guidelines at home. Learning to respect the rules is part of the growing up process. Children may express their dislike for those rules, but they will not hate you for enforcing them. Some children interpret a lack of rules as their parents not caring about them at all.

In my house, I first set my children's bedtime for 8:30 p.m., and they hated it. They would argue that none of their friends had to go to bed that early, so after a while I cut them some slack and pushed it back to 9:15. They still were not happy. I felt that this was late enough for them to stay up, so I stood my ground, and as much as they didn't like it, eventually they got used to it, and now it doesn't even faze them. They have gotten so used to going to bed at 9:15 on weekdays that even on weekends they find themselves going to bed early, because they are too tired to stay up later, even when they try to. I don't even have to say "it's time to go to bed" to them anymore; when the clock strikes a quarter after nine, they turn the lights off and get right in the bed. It has become a part of their daily routine, and they take pride in being responsible and getting in bed on time without my having to tell them.

Our children follow a schedule in school with no complaints. They eat lunch at a certain time, they have gym at a certain time, and every other subject at the scheduled time. They can't go to lunch whenever they feel like it; it doesn't work that way. So why can't they follow a schedule at home, as well? All you have to do is continue the pattern at home, set a dinner time, the same time every night or as close to it as possible, and set a bedtime. You can give a little leniency on the weekends to relax them and to keep them from getting frustrated or feeling as if they are in the military. This will help keep them focused and well-rested during the week, so they can concentrate better on their schoolwork.

As adults, we still follow guidelines and schedules. We don't, for the most part, stay up until the wee hours of the morning when we know we have to get up at 6:00 a.m. or earlier to go to work. We try to go to bed at a reasonable hour so we can get enough rest to feel refreshed the next morning. Now, we may slip up once in a while and stay at that party until 2:00 a.m. when we know we have to go to work in a few hours, but we don't do it every night. It's okay to make the occasional exception. The point is, as adults, we condition ourselves and make these sacrifices because we know what's best for us. Children, however, don't know what is best for them most of the time. That's why it's your job to let them know, by setting the rules and schedules for them. Don't worry that they complain; they will understand and thank you when they get older.

Some behavior problems stem from children simply seeking attention from their parents or loved ones. Interact with your children, play family games, let them help you in the kitchen so they feel important to the family. You have to stay involved in your children's lives every day. Don't just let them play all day without your being involved at some point. President Barack Obama said it best when he said, "In the end, there is no program or policy that can substitute for a parent—for a mother or father who will attend those parent/teacher conferences or help with homework or turn off the TV, put away the video games, read to their child. I speak to you not just as a president, but as a father, when I say the responsibility for our children's education must begin at home." So talk to your child's teacher, find out what your child is like in school, because a lot of the time children act totally different in school than they do at home, seeking attention from classmates because they don't get enough at home. Stop faulting the teachers when you don't even take the time to find out what is going on in the classroom. If you show your child that you are on the same page as his teacher, he will know there is nothing he can get away with.

Keeping the doors of communication open with your child's teacher will make a world of difference. Our children spend as much time in school as they do at home, if not more, and when they come home, they want to share their day with you. Take the time to listen, and let them know that you care. It's not enough to just drop your kids off at school in the morning and pick them up at the end of the school day and think your job is done. You have to get involved.

We can't continue to ignore our children. We have to ask ourselves, what future do I want for my children? And then we need to help them work toward obtaining the goals we have set, in the best way we can. We make sacrifices every day for things that are far less important. When are we going to start making sacrifices for the children we brought into this world? I say, make that commitment and start right now, because tomorrow is not promised to anyone.

LaVergne, TN USA
05 December 2010
207463LV00001B/6/P